by **Anne O'Brien**
illustrated by **Nancy Carpenter**

Chapters

The Diary. 2

The Names. 9

Leialoha's Family 12

⬱Harcourt

Orlando   Boston   Dallas   Chicago   San Diego

Visit *The Learning Site!*

www.harcourtschool.com

The Diary

They found the diary in an old trunk. It was in the shadows at the back of the carriage house at the edge of camp.

"Are we supposed to be in here?" Toshi asked when they first went in, gazing about in the dim light. There were boxes and piles of old furniture stacked along the walls.

"They said we could look anywhere as long as we didn't leave camp," Nani said. "It's the perfect place to find something old, which is the next-to-last thing on our list."

"Go, team!" said Josh. "We are going to win this scavenger hunt!"

Toshi lifted the lid on the old trunk. Annabelle's eyes got wide when she saw what was inside it.

"Hey, check this out, everyone," she called. She ran over to the trunk and held up a book covered in brown leather. "This sure looks ancient." The others gathered around as she lifted the cover and read the first page. There, in flowery, old-fashioned writing, was an inscription:

DIARY

Leialoha Kahaluwai

1897-1899

"Whoa," said Josh, scratching his head with one hand. "This is seriously old. How is this name pronounced?"

"Leh-ee-uh-LO-ha is the first name," said Nani.

Annabelle opened the diary to a page of writing, squinted at the elaborate cursive, and began to read, "Ninth November, eighteen ninety-seven. We have just returned from such an exciting outing. In honor of the occasion, Mrs. King marched the entire school down to the docks to witness the arrival of our Princess Ka'iulani [kə·ē·ōō·lah´·nē] returning home from study abroad. I was only four years old when she left, so I have only heard stories of her."

"Wow, Princess Ka'iulani!" said Nani. "That's back when Hawaii still had kings and queens!"

"We should be careful handling those pages," said Josh. "They look pretty dry and brittle."

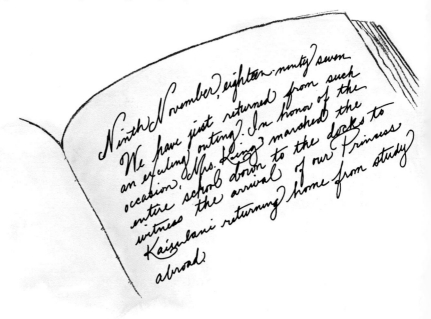

"Keep reading," said Toshi.

"How loud were the cheers when the ship docked and the people first saw her, waving from the upper deck," Annabelle read. "Later, her carriage drove right past where we were standing, and she looked right at me! She is so beautiful and smiled so warmly and sweetly at us all. We all have hope in our hearts that now she is home, Hawaii may be ours once again." The four campers looked at each other, their eyes wide.

"This is like . . . real history!" Josh said.

"We've got to show it to Ken and Hana," Toshi said.

"I bet we found the best old thing of all!" said Nani.

When they got to Ken and Hana, the camp counselors, everyone started talking at once.

"Wait, wait," said Hana, "one at a time. Okay, Nani, you first. What's up?"

"We went into the carriage house, looking for something old, and Annabelle found this book in an old trunk. It's a diary and it's more than a hundred years old!" exclaimed Nani.

"It might be very valuable," said Toshi. "We should try to find the person it belongs to."

"It talks about Princess Ka'iulani, the day she came back to Hawaii from studying abroad," said Josh.

"Listen," said Annabelle, opening the diary again to the page about Princess Ka'iulani. When she finished reading, Ken and Hana were wide-eyed, too.

Annabelle turned to another page and continued reading, as everyone listened attentively.

"Twentieth April, eighteen ninety-eight. Emma Peterson, Mapuana Grover, Michiko Nakamura, and I walked home together, as we always do. We stopped at the Nakamuras' store, and Michiko's father gave us each a piece of candy. Then Michiko's brother Kazuo came into the store. He is usually away at school. He is so handsome that we all began to giggle when he spoke to us, except for Michiko, of course!"

"This really is a find," Ken said. "I think Toshi is right—the diary could be very valuable to someone. That last reading gives me an idea of how we might find the owner."

"But Lcialuhia, who wrote the diary, would be over a hundred years old now," said Nani.

"I'm sure she's no longer living," said Hana, "but perhaps we could find some of her relatives."

"Here's my idea for finding the owner," said Ken. "Whenever you four have some free time, why don't you read the diary and make notes. I think the most important details will be the names, like Kahalewai and Nakamura."

Leialoha Kahalewai - born March 4, 1885
Friends:
Emma Peterson
Mapuana Grover
Michiko Nakamura
Kazuo Nakamura - Michiko's brother
Mr. Nakamura - Michiko's father
School mistress:
Mrs. King

The Names

Over the next week of camp, Annabelle, Nani, Toshi,
and Josh got together whenever they could. They made
lists of all the names Leialoha mentioned. They found out
how old Leialoha was from an entry she made the day of
her thirteenth birthday. They also learned more about
Leialoha's life:

"Sixth May, eighteen ninety-eight. The rehearsals are
going well, and Mrs. King says our pageant will be a
splendid success. I am playing the part of King Kalakaua. I
like him so much because he brought back our old
Hawaiian customs, which the missionaries had banned
and said were barbaric—even the hula and the luau!
What is barbaric about a dance and a feast?"

After they'd read the whole diary, they met with Ken and Hana to make a plan. Ken started them off by saying, "Okay, team, what ideas do we have for finding these people?"

"How about the phone book?" asked Josh.

"Could we look them up on the Internet?" Nani asked.

"We could ask older people if they've ever heard of any of these names," Toshi said.

"My grandmother went to the library to look up some information about our family in a book," Annabelle said. "Maybe there are books with some of these names in them."

By the end of their meeting, they were divided into smaller teams and ready to go.

At the next meeting, Josh and Toshi had the phone book, but they'd had a troublesome time with it. There were so many listings under every family name—especially Peterson, Grover, Nakamura, and King—that they didn't know where to start. Hana had taken Annabelle to the library after camp one afternoon. They brought back what they'd found: a book that mentioned the Nakamuras' store and a short historical account of the girls' school Leialoha attended in Honolulu, headed by Mrs. King. In the meantime, Ken and Nani had been on the computer tracing the Kahalewai family.

Leialoha's Family

"Guess what we found out," Nani said, barely able to contain her excitement. "Leialoha married Kazuo Nakamura!"

"I think he might have become a doctor!" Josh added. "You know how we were all supposed to talk to our families? Well, my grandmother remembers a Doctor Kazuo Nakamura from when she worked at the naval hospital. He was retired, but he used to come in to teach."

On the computer screen Nani and Ken showed the chart they'd found of the Kahalewai family. There were the names—Leialoha and Kazuo Nakamura. They had five children and fourteen grandchildren.

Checking back and forth between the computer and the phone book, they finally found a match. Kalani Nakamura, a grandson of Leialoha and Kazuo, was listed in the phone book. Was he the right person? It was time to make a phone call.

"It should be Annabelle," Nani said. "She's the one who found the diary."

Annabelle picked up the phone and punched in the number. Everyone listened, restless with anticipation.

"Hello, is this Mr. Kalani Nakamura?" Annabelle asked. "Are you the grandson of Leialoha and Kazuo Nakamura?" She nodded at her friends, her eyes dancing.

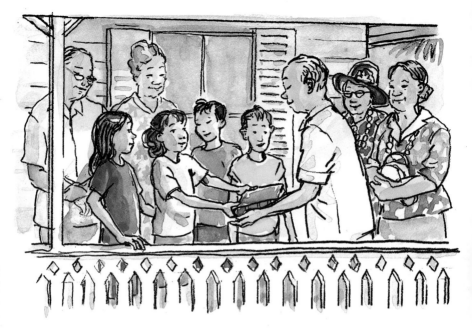

Mr. Nakamura was so happy to hear about the diary that he invited them all to dinner the next night. Ken and Hana drove the team to Mr. Nakamura's house after camp. The house was small and neat, surrounded by tropical flowers. Mr. Nakamura came to the gate and ushered them onto the lanai, the wraparound porch. It was full of people! One by one, he introduced the children to his sisters, brothers, and cousins, all descendants of Leialoha and Kazuo Nakamura. Annabelle stepped forward and held out the book covered in brown leather.

"Here is your grandmother's diary that we found in the carriage house at Camp Makanikai," she said.

It was a wonderful evening. They all sat together in the tropical air, eating and listening as Mr. Nakamura read parts of the diary. Leialoha's grandchildren laughed and cried as their grandmother's stories filled the air. They remembered other stories of their family, of Princess Ka'iulani, of Hawaii's history. Everyone wanted to hear how the book was found and how the children had found Leialoha's family.

When it was time to leave, everyone felt that they'd made many new friends. Each one of the Nakamuras shook the children's hands and thanked them for bringing the diary.

"Just think of us walking into that carriage house," said Nani, as Ken drove them toward home. "We had no idea what was going to happen to us!"

"You did something really important," Hana said. "You gave that family a piece of their history back."

"We never imagined we'd learn so much," said Toshi.

"I don't even remember who won the scavenger hunt that day," said Josh, "but we're the ones who found the real treasure."

Annabelle smiled and said, "And we're the ones who got the prize!"